Li'l Sis and Uncle Willie

A Story Based on the Life and Paintings of William H. Johnson

Gwen Everett

National Museum of
American Art
Smithsonian Institution
Washington, D.C.

Hyperion Paperbacks
for Children
New York

I remember the day Uncle Willie came home. It was a hot June afternoon in Florence, South Carolina.

Everyone left off their work around the farmyard when they heard my grandma, Mom Alice, yell, "He's here! He's here!" We all knew she was talking about Uncle Willie. He'd been away for years and years. After moving to New York as a young man to study art, he had traveled to Scandinavia, France, Germany, and North Africa to live and paint.

Now, there he was, home for a visit, standing with his hands on his hips, and laughing. He had wavy hair and skin the color of light brown sugar. As I stared up at him, I thought I had never seen anyone so tall. Suddenly, he swept me up in a big bear hug.

Calendar

"I'm your Uncle Willie," he said with a smile.

"I'm Li'l Sis. I'm almost six and this is my doll, Lillian. We go everywhere together," I said.

When he smiled at Lillian, I knew we had found a best friend.

That night it was so hot Lillian and I couldn't sleep. We went to the kitchen for a glass of water. No one was awake but Uncle Willie. He was unpacking some of his paintings and said we could stay and watch.

As he unrolled them, he told us that people all over Europe and the United States bought his paintings, but it had not been easy for him to become an artist. He had studied for many years at an art school in New York called the National Academy of Design. There he learned how to mix paints and use a brush to make the things he painted look real.

Then he showed us his painting of the old, rickety Jacobi Hotel. Lillian and I thought it looked haunted, and Uncle Willie had to tell us stories so we wouldn't be afraid.

Lillian's favorite stories were about the black people of Harlem, a part of New York City. We could hardly imagine the men and women Uncle Willie told us about who wore big hats, long gloves, and pointy shoes of different colors. He would paint them talking at cafe tables, playing music on street corners, or dancing the jitterbug. We'd never heard of anything like this before.

Uncle Willie showed us the steps to the jitterbug. Lillian loved it. I would whirl around and throw her in the air. Uncle Willie said, "You dance so fine, you could become as famous some day as Josephine Baker who dances in Paris."

Uncle Willie could give me dreams as bright as the pictures he painted.

We passed some workers in the cotton fields the next day. Uncle Willie said he didn't think he would ever forget what it was like to pick cotton—rising before dawn, sore hands, aching back, and always, the hot sun! Staring off into the horizon, he added, "People in the city don't plow the fields, feed chickens, or even grow cotton. In New York, there are no farms and people live in tall buildings. Pavement is everywhere and there isn't much grass." I thought maybe he was joking with me, because I had never been anywhere except Florence. But the look in his eyes told me that he was remembering, not making up stories.

Calendar

W.H.Johnson

Maybe New York wasn't such a fun place after all. "Where do children play in New York if there aren't any fields or green grass?" I asked. Uncle Willie told me that children play together on playgrounds, on sidewalks, and even in the streets. Sometimes, they play ring games and sing rhymes.

Little Sallie Water,
Sitting in the Saucer,
Rise, Sallie, rise,
Wipe your weeping eyes.
Put your hands on your hips
and let your backbone slip.
Shake it to the east, Sallie,
Shake it to the west, Sallie,
Shake it to the very one that
you love the best.

Calendar

Lillian and I liked that song a lot. We wanted to sing it all the way to church on Sunday, but Mom Alice wouldn't let us. I remember that day because we had a baptism in the river.

As Reverend Brown blessed the people in the water, we stood on the bank and sang. I can still hear Uncle Willie's strong, deep voice singing,

Swing low, sweet chariot,
comin' for to carry me home.

Standing beside him near the water, I felt sad and held Lillian very tightly. I knew Uncle Willie would leave that day for New York. He wanted to go back to his home in Denmark.

The day after Uncle Willie left, Lillian and I were very unhappy, so we went to visit Aunt Della. I thought of how much both Lillian and I liked to hear the iron hiss when Aunt Della sprinkled water on it. "Maybe this will cheer us up," I told Lillian. It didn't though.

"Why can't I go to New York to see Uncle Willie before he leaves?" I asked Aunt Della. "I'll be six in another month, and Mom Alice even said I'm old enough to go to market with her to sell eggs."

I was very excited, talking so fast the words tumbled out. "If I could just get on the train in Florence today, Uncle Willie could show me and Lillian all those places he told us about before he leaves on the ship to Denmark. I promise I'll come home soon."

W.H. Johnson

Aunt Della laughed, then said in a serious voice, "I expect you'll be making your own decisions soon enough, Li'l Sis. Willie only told you and Lillian about the fun. He didn't tell you about how crowded it is in the city. Sometimes it seems like too many people living in one space can cause them to become angry enough to fight. Just last summer, a crowd broke windows, turned over cars, started fires, and looted stores when they thought a white policeman had shot and killed a black soldier."

I asked Aunt Della if that was why Uncle Willie moved to Europe. She said, "Uncle Willie first went to Europe to study art, but he liked living there because people were friendlier to black people."

After this, Lillian and I didn't feel quite so bad about not going to New York.

Uncle Willie wrote that he arrived in Europe safely. This letter joined others in my scrapbook of letters, postcards, and photographs he had sent home. He told me how happy he and his wife Holcha were. I could almost smell the salt air in the harbor and the apple blossoms in spring when he described Kerteminde, the town where he lived in Denmark. The snapshots Uncle Willie sent were my favorites. One showed Uncle Willie painting on the sidewalk in Paris. It reminded me of how he said he painted the Jacobi Hotel.

Lillian and I decided to save the pennies I earned at the market selling eggs so we could surprise Uncle Willie with a visit the next summer.

Uncle Willie looking at a painting with the American ambassador to Sweden!

Uncle Willie called this man "Old Salt," but I think it was because I couldn't pronounce his real name.

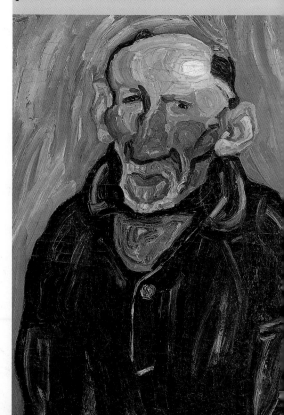

Spring time in Kerteminde

Uncle Willie dressed as an
Arab when he was in Africa

Aunt Holcha weaving in a
room filled with Uncle
Willie's paintings.

Uncle Willie called this "Still
Life," but I always thought of
it as lunch.

Uncle Willie painting in
Paris.

But before Lillian and I could save enough money to go to Europe, something terrible happened. World War II. Nazi soldiers invaded Poland. The Japanese bombed Pearl Harbor and America went to war. Mom Alice read to me about the black men and women who joined the army. One soldier named Dorie Miller shot down four Japanese planes at Pearl Harbor. He wasn't even trained in how to shoot a machine gun.

As soon as I heard that, I wrote to Uncle Willie and told him I was going to join the Red Cross and come to Europe to help him. But he and Holcha had already decided it wasn't safe for them there and had returned to New York.

Similar one in Calendar

AMERICAN RED CROSS

W.H.Johnson.

Uncle Willie continued to write Lillian and me from New York. He told us that Harlem was full of artists and writers and musicians who were black. He sent me snapshots of new paintings he had made about famous black Americans. He said it was important for us to know the roles we played in history.

He told me to remember people like Nat Turner, who led one of the first slave rebellions in Virginia, and was later hanged for it. He explained how people like Harriet Tubman led hundreds of slaves to freedom on the Underground Railroad. It wasn't a real railroad, but escaped slaves used secret routes to move from house to house, church to church, and through the woods, until they reached freedom in the North.

These pictures of his paintings joined others in my scrapbook. They made me feel proud to be an African American.

As time passed, my grandmother grew older and the two of us often talked about how much we wished Uncle Willie would come back to visit. But he never did. He continued to write me about his paintings and his life, and I would always share these with Mom Alice and Aunt Della. When he wrote that Holcha had died, I wished I could have been with him to tell him how sorry I felt.

One day, though, I realized his letters had stopped. That afternoon, as Mom Alice sat in her rocker petting one of her naughty cats, I asked her why Uncle Willie would stop writing me. She sighed and smiled sadly. She said it was difficult for Uncle Willie after Holcha died. He grew confused and didn't seem to want to live without her. He had to be sent to a hospital so a doctor could look after him. He never got better and had to stay in the hospital for the rest of his life.

The day Mom Alice told me Uncle Willie had died, I took Lillian down from the shelf where I kept her now. For the first time in years, I hugged her the way Uncle Willie had hugged me so long ago.

And, I remembered that Sunday on the river bank when he sang so sadly with faraway eyes.

Swing low, sweet chariot,
Comin' for to carry me home,
Swing low, sweet chariot,
Comin' for to carry me home.
I look'd over Jordan and what did I see,
Comin' for to carry me home,
A band of angels comin' after me,
Comin' for to carry me home.

W.H.Joh

Today, I often look through the scrapbook I started when I was five. I remember how Uncle Willie taught me to paste in the pictures and write about them. I remember how I felt when he painted Lillian and me with my flyswatter, just like a grown-up.

Even though he's been gone for years, I'm sure he would be happy to know his paintings still remind us of who we are and what we can achieve. They keep Uncle Willie's memory as bright as the colors in his paintings—for me and for all of us.

I will always remember that special summer when Uncle Willie came home.

Me and Lillian

Going to church

Our neighbors down the road

...verend Brown

Aunt Della's husband going to the market where I sold my eggs.

Uncle Willie when he was first in New York

Chain gangs used to work on the roads around our house.

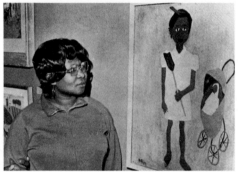

Ernestine Margaret Brown, the "real life" Li'l Sis, at an exhibition of Johnson's work in 1971.

Illustrations: Cover, p.5, p.31 *Li'l Sis*; p.1 *Self-Portrait with Pipe*; p.3 *Early Morning Work*; p.4 *Self-Portrait*; p.7 *Jacobia Hotel*; p.8 *Cafe and Street Musicians*; p.9 *Jitterbugs (I)*; p.11 *Cotton Pickers*; p.12 *New York Skyline at Night*; p.13 *Children Playing at Dockside*; p.14 *I Baptize Thee*; p.17 *Woman Ironing*; p.18 *Moon Over Harlem*; p.21 Scrapbook I (clockwise): *Mountain Blossoms*; *Still Life*; *Old Salt, Denmark*; p.23 *Red Cross Nurses Handing Out Wool*; p.24 *Nat Turner*; p.25 *Underground Railroad*; p.27 *Mom and Dad*; p.29 *Swing Low, Sweet Chariot*; p.31 Scrapbook II (clockwise): *Man in a Vest*; *Three Little Children*; *Self-Portrait*; *Chain Gang*; *Going to Market*; *Going to Church*.

Special thanks to Claudine Brown, Wendy Byrne, Schroeder Cherry, Zora Felton, Robert Hall, Amy Hollander, Harry Jackson, Wendy Lukehart, Chuck Mikolaycak, Lynn Russell, Maria Salvador, Robert San Souci and Mary Ellen Wilson.

Li'l Sis and Uncle Willie is a fictional story based on the actual events in the life of William H. Johnson, whose paintings are the artwork for this book. The National Museum of American Art in Washington, D.C., has preserved more than one thousand of Johnson's paintings. Older readers who wish to learn more about this artist should read *Homecoming: The Art and Life of William H. Johnson* by Richard J. Powell, whose support and research are gratefully acknowledged.

For Jason   For Keel
—G.E.   —S.D.

First Hyperion Paperback edition: September 1994
1   3   5   7   9   10   8   6   4   2

Concept and design: Steve Dietz
Editorial Assistant: Deborah Thomas
Jacket and title page design: Christy Hale

The National Museum of American Art, Smithsonian Institution, is dedicated to the preservation, exhibition, and study of the visual arts in America. The museum, whose publications program also includes the scholarly journal *American Art*, has extensive research resources: the databases of the Inventories of American Painting and Sculpture, several image archives, and a variety of scholarly fellowships. For more information or a catalogue of publications, write: Office of Publications, National Museum of Art, Smithsonian Institution, Washington, DC 20560.

This publication is made possible with the support of the Sara Roby Foundation.

Printed in Hong Kong by South China Printing Co.

Library of Congress Cataloging-in-Publication Data

Everett, Gwen.
    Li'l Sis and Uncle Willie: a story based on the life and paintings of William H. Johnson / by Gwen Everett — 1st Hyperion Paperback ed.
        p.   cm.
    "National Museum of American Art, Smithsonian Institution, Washington, D.C."
    ISBN 1-56282-593-3
    1. Johnson, William H., 1901–70—Juvenile literature.   2. Afro-American painters—Biography—Juvenile literature.   [1. Johnson, William H., 1901–70. 2. Artists.   3. Afro-Americans—Biography. 4. Painting, American.]   I. National Museum of American Art (U.S.).   II. Title.
    ND237.J73E94   1994
    759.13—dc20   94-2455
                                                                                    CIP
                                                                                    AC